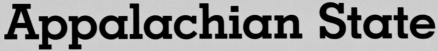

Appalachian State
A TO Z

Written by
Anne Aldridge Webb

Illustrated by
Laurie Bostian

Available from:

Parkway Publishers, Inc.

P. O. Box 3678, Boone, North Carolina 28607

Telephone/Facsimile: (828) 265-3993

www.parkwaypublishers.com

Library of Congress Cataloging-in-Publication Data

Webb, Anne Aldridge.
Appalachian State, A to Z / by Anne Aldridge Webb ; Illustrated by
Laurie Bostian.
p. cm.
ISBN 978-1-933251-69-1
1. Appalachian State University--Juvenile literature. 2. Alphabet books--
Juvenile literature. I. Bostian, Laurie, ill. II. Title.
LD173.W43 2010
378.756'843--dc22
2009029804

We gratefully acknowledge the permission of
Appalachian State University for the use of its trademarks.

Printed by:

RR Donnelley

Reynosa, Mexico

First Printing October 2009

To Jackson, Judge and Phillip,

We hope you love college as much
as your mamas did, and enjoy learning
as much as we always will.

What we learn with pleasure we never forget.
—*Alfred Mercier*

Aa

A is for Appalachian
Appalachian is the name of a school
and the mountain range nearby,
a beautiful place for students to learn
in the Carolina hilltops so high.

Bb

B is for Blowing Rock
Did you know there is a place
where snow goes up, not down?
It's the gorgeous Blowing Rock
near Appalachian State's hometown.

Cc

C is for Crafts
Crafts and other types of folk art
get serious study at ASU.
They demonstrate local culture;
they are lovely and valuable too.

Dd

D is for Daniel Boone
The town of Boone gets its name
from a famous pioneer.
Townspeople and students alike
proudly exclaim "Daniel Boone lived here."

Ee

E is for Environment
Students study the environment
paying attention to land, water and air.
Trying to improve our natural world,
they care about our future welfare.

Ff

F is for First
Many students become teachers;
going to North Carolina schools to educate.
In number of teachers trained each year,
Appalachian ranks first in the state.

Gg

G is for Graduate
When all studies are finally done
students march in to graduate.
Wearing black and gold caps and gowns,
they get ready to celebrate.

Hh

H is for Hike

Through dense forests and open fields
by waterfalls and sparkling creeks,
students take many nature hikes
to the tops of mountain peaks.

Ii

I is for Ice

When walking on winter mornings
students must heed this advice,
be careful on sidewalks as you go to class
for they may be covered in ice.

Jj

J is for Jump
To jump in the duck pond for "Polar Plunge"
brings on a tremendous thrill.
Students do this to raise money for charity
each winter as they fight the chill.

Kk

K is for Kidd Brewer Stadium

Kidd Brewer Stadium on a football Saturday
is filled with excited, cheering Mountaineers.
Nicknamed "The Rock" by the fans who love it;
it has seen many victories through the years.

Ll

L is for Library

Where can you learn about trains and race cars?
What has over 800,000 books?
The answer is the Carol Belk Library;
settle into one of its cozy nooks.

Mm

M is for Music

Music students can learn to make CDs
or work at a radio station.
They can become top notch musicians,
as part of their ASU music education.

Nn

N is for National Champions
More than one, and more than two
the Mountaineers can celebrate,
as national championships keep coming
their football legacy grows strong and great.

Oo

O is for Old Mountain Jug
The Old Mountain Jug is a cool trophy
that Appalachian can win each year,
if the team defeats Western Carolina
leaving fans grinning from ear to ear.

Pp

P is for Play
Students go see the Horn In the West,
a play that is known worldwide.
It tells the story of mountain settlers
and takes place on a stage outside.

Qq

Q is for Quinn Center
The Quinn Center is a spot on campus
to have fun and to exercise.
Healthy bodies are very important,
for students to be truly wise.

Rr

R is for Ride

It's hard to walk across a campus so large
so the students do something smart,
They hop on a bus with a funny name.
It's called ASU's Appalcart.

Ss

S is for Snowskiing
Imagine skiing as part of a class,
a physical education grade to earn.
At ASU they swish down the slopes,
and have great fun as they learn.

Tt

T is for Tailgate
Before football games on Saturdays
the fans find it hard to wait;
so they picnic together at "The Rock"
at a fun party called a tailgate.

Uu

U is for University
Appalachian was started by the Dougherty brothers,
their first names were B.B. and D.D.
What began as a school to train local students
is now a top university.

Vv

V is for View
The top of Howard's Knob
has a magnificent view to show,
tall surrounding mountains
and the ASU campus below.

Ww

W is for Wind
Wind is a powerful force
as some ASU scientists know,
they use mountain wind turbines
to make energy out of airflow.

Xx

X is for X marks the spot
X marks the spot for this place to learn;
a space of meaning, beauty and worth.
It was said the campus appeared to be
"the face of all heaven come to earth."

Yy

Y is for Yosef
Wearing a big black hat and overalls,
Yosef is a mountain man so true.
He represents alumni and students
as the dear mascot for ASU.

Zz

Z is for Zzzzz
Zzzz is the sweet and sleepy sound
as this little one dreams away,
of going to Appalachian
to become a student someday.

AFTERWORD

Some interesting facts about Appalachian State University and the themes included in this book are shared by Pat Farthing, a Watauga County native and long time librarian for a special collection in the university library.

The Dougherty brothers had a worthy goal in mind when they established Watauga Academy in Boone, North Carolina. They wanted to train young men and women to become teachers in their local mountain communities. The Academy opened its doors in 1899 with 53 students. In the 100+ years since, this institution has undergone many changes as it grew from a teacher training school to a teachers college and to its current status as an outstanding comprehensive university in the Southeast and the nation.

"YOSEF," as in "do it yourself." The people who settled the Blue Ridge range of the Appalachian Mountains have always been a fiercely independent people, taking pride in their accomplishments and ability to achieve on their own. It was this pride that led the Dougherty brothers to establish the first teacher training school in Northwestern North Carolina. And it was this same pride that led Appalachian students, in the 1940's, to choose as their mascot the strong, independent mountaineer, so full of enthusiastic school spirit, whom they named, in typical mountain dialect, Yosef.